SCUOLA D'ING
storie per bambini di

the three Billy Goats Gruff

GIUNTIJunior

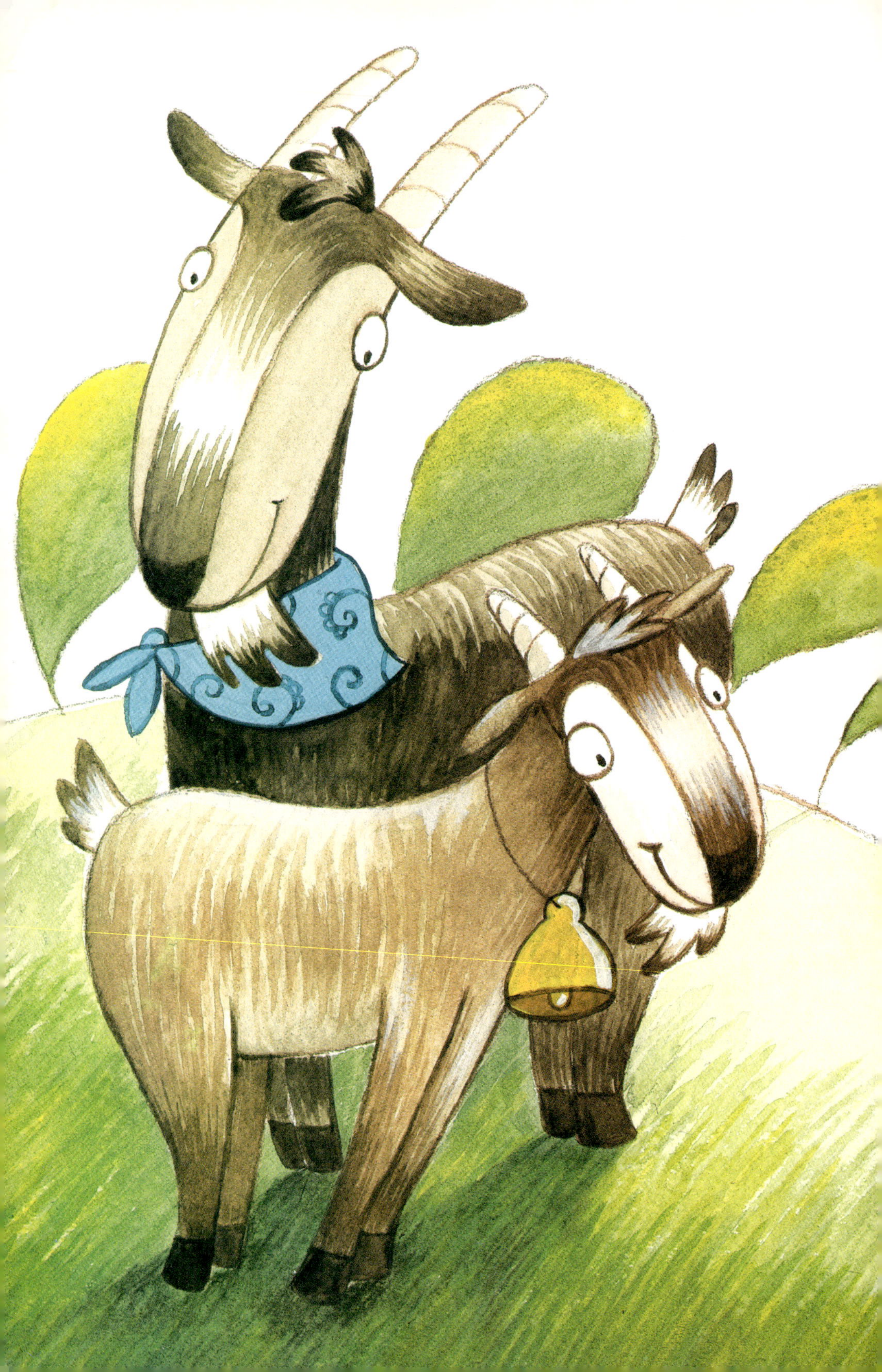

This is the story of the three Billy Goats Gruff: Big Goat, Middle-sized Goat and Little Goat.

They live in a barn.

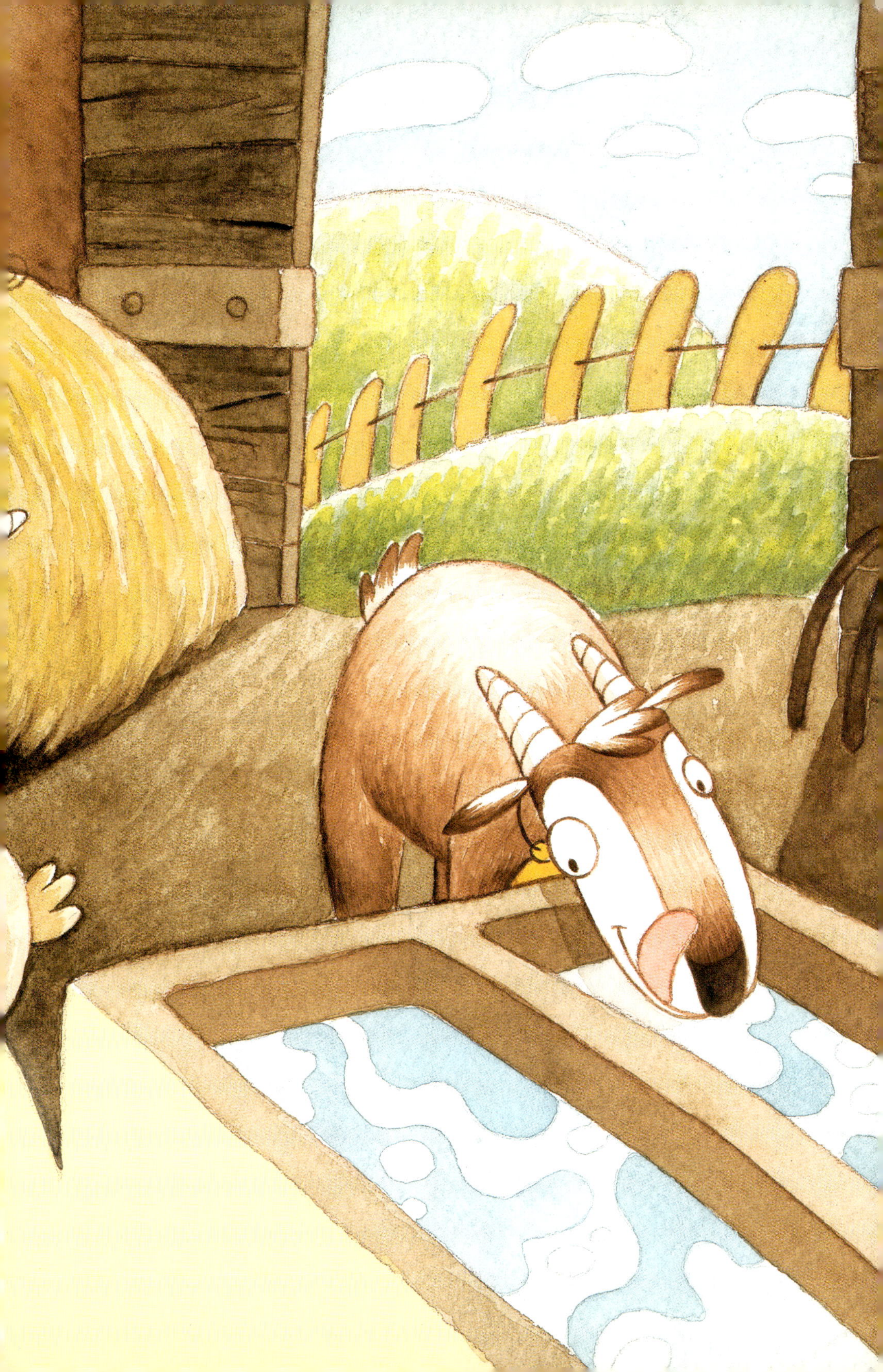

One day they decide
to go and eat some grass
in the field.

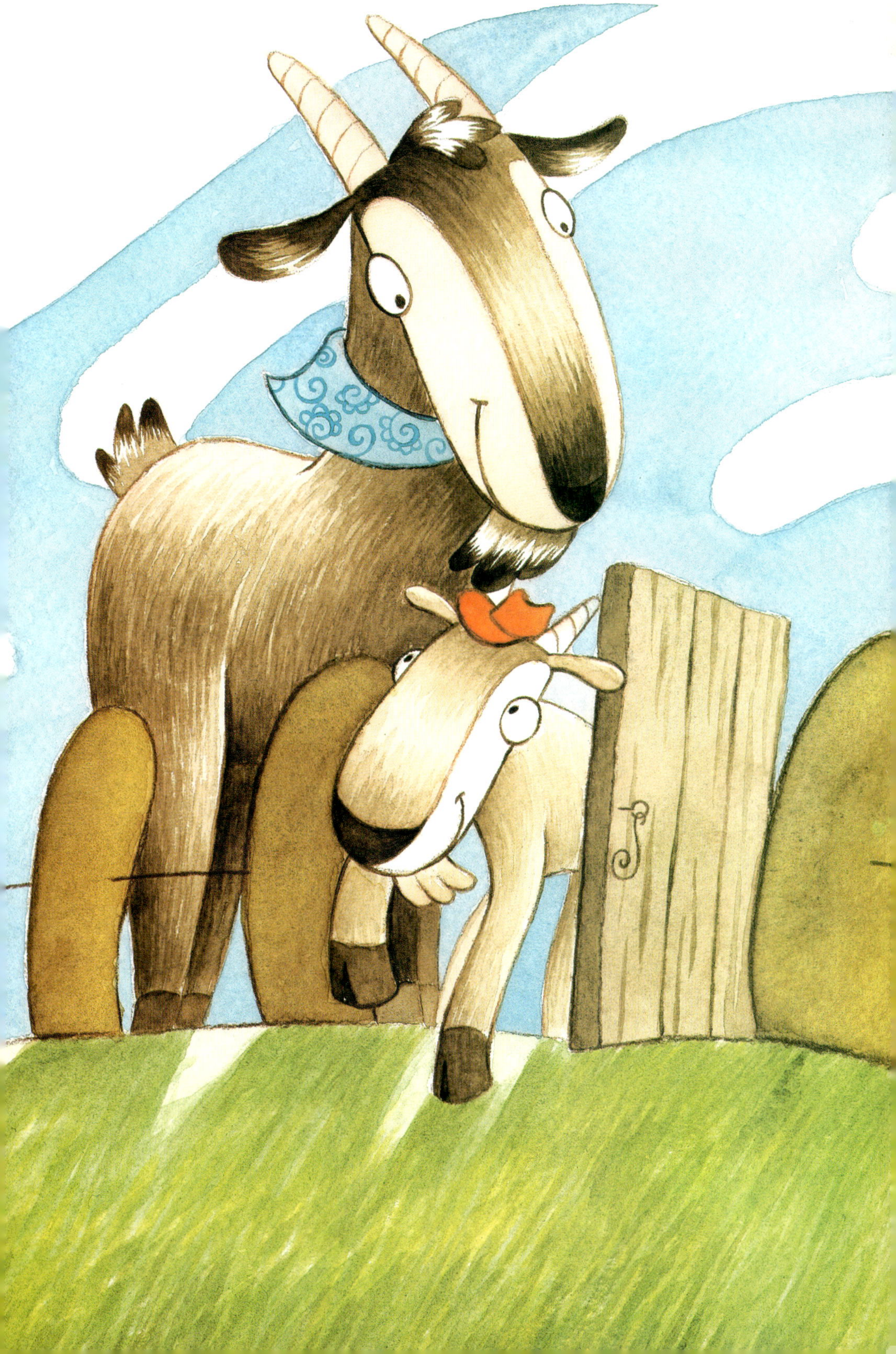

On the way they have to cross a bridge, but...

... under the bridge lives
a terrible, ugly giant.

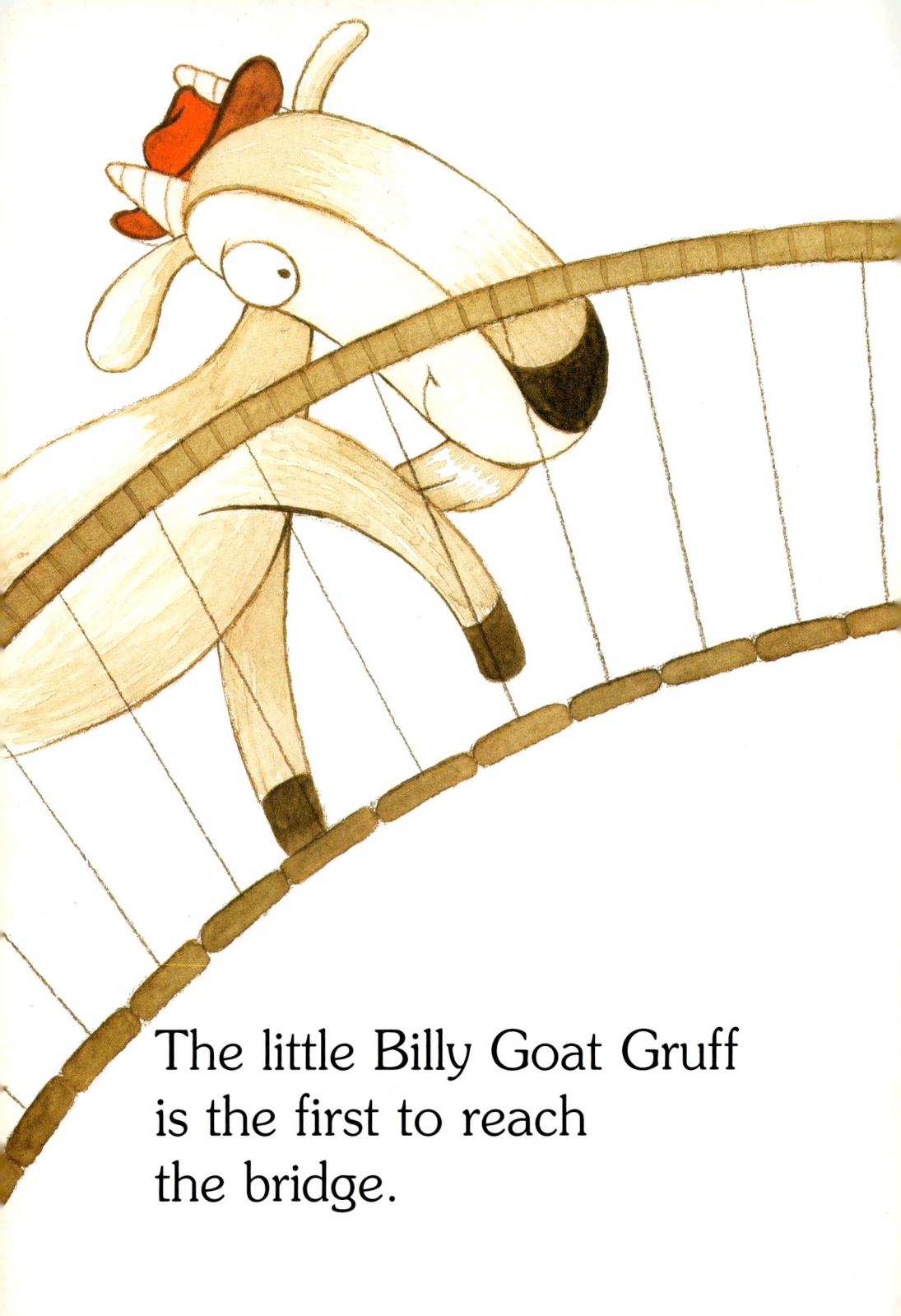

The little Billy Goat Gruff
is the first to reach
the bridge.

Trippity-trop!
Trippity-trop!

– Who's that crossing my bridge? – growls the giant.

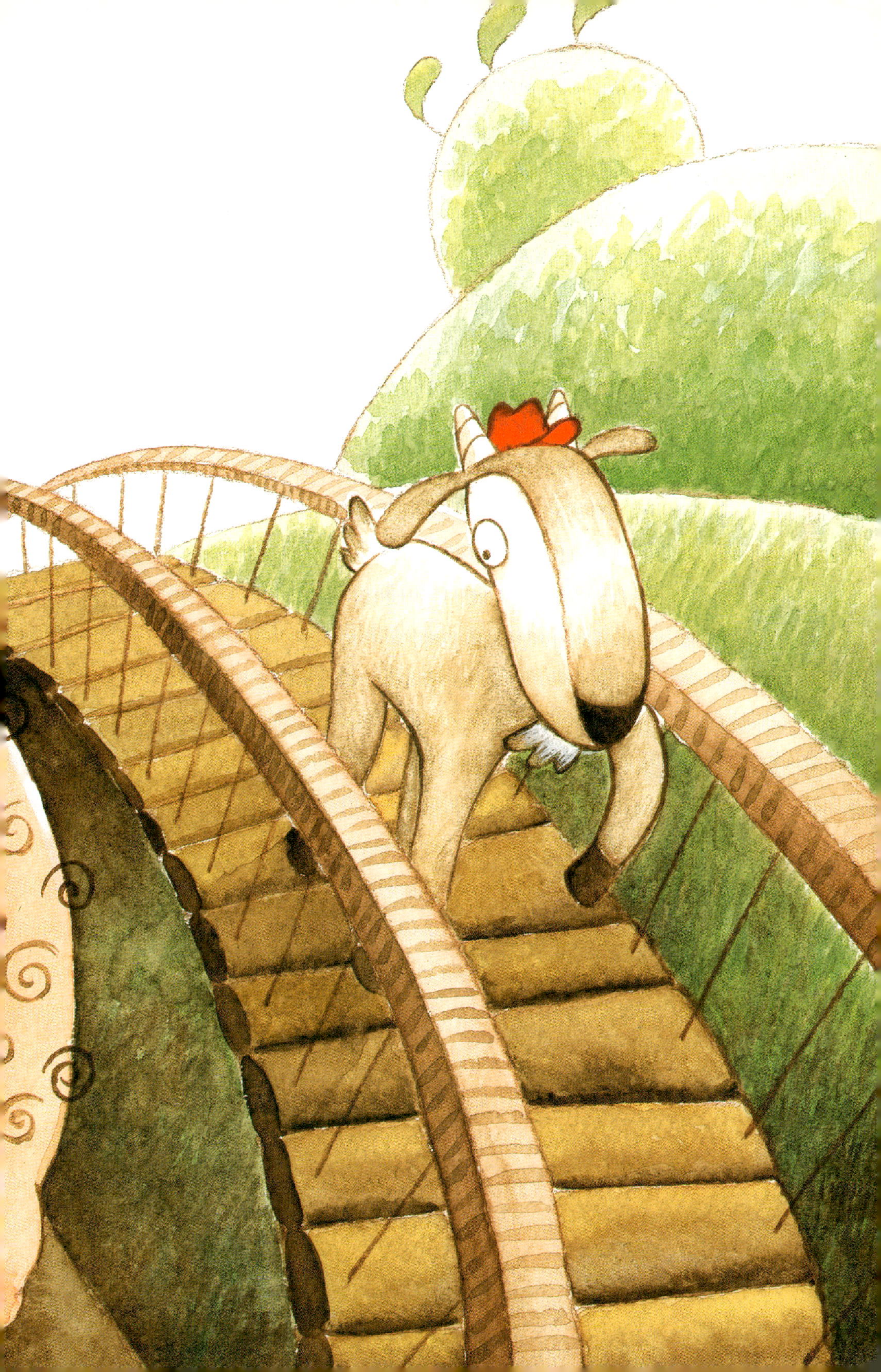

– Billy Goat Gruff – says the little goat in his tiny voice.

– I'm going to the field to eat some grass.

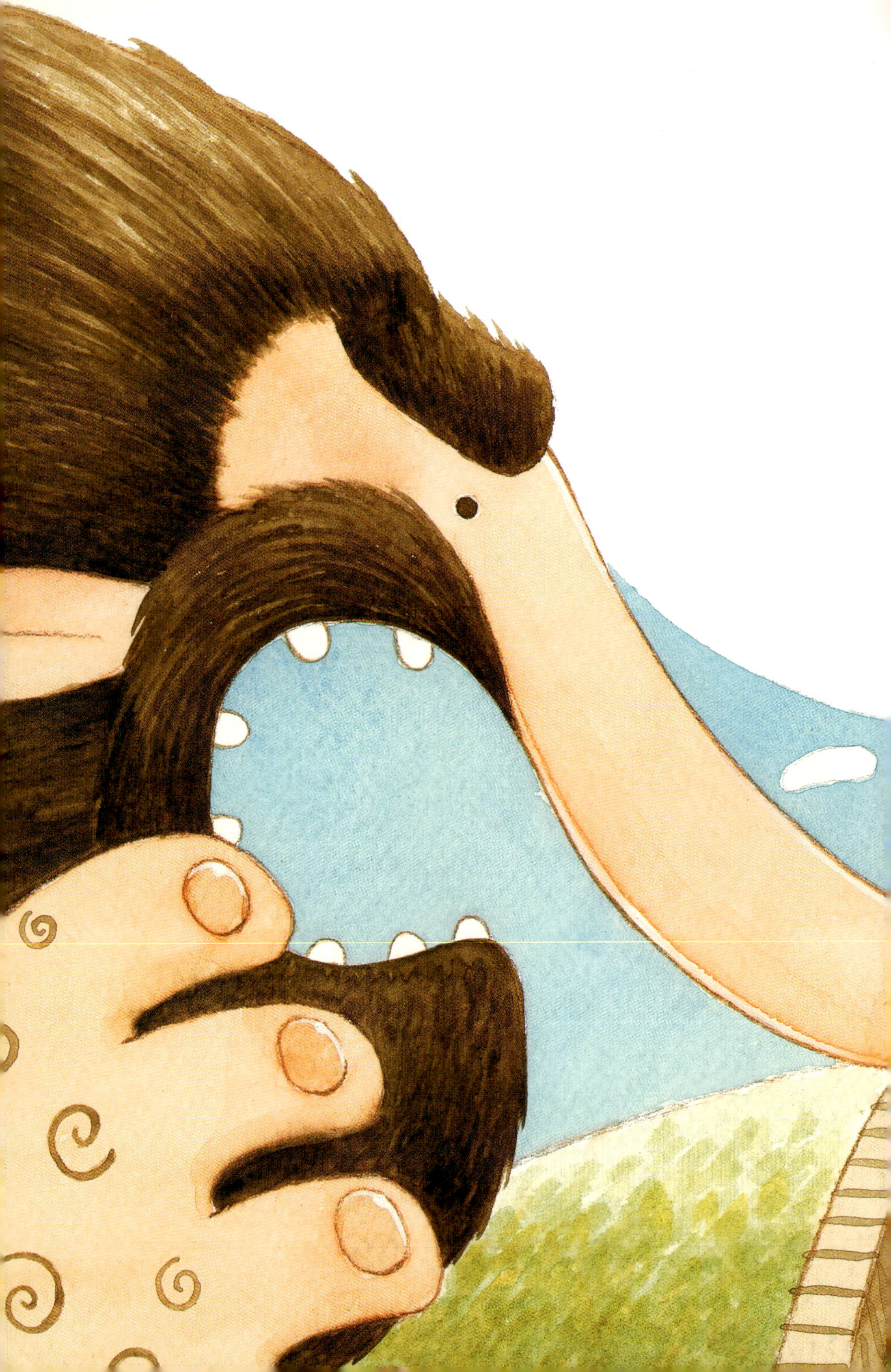

– Oh no, you're not! –
says the giant.
– I'm going to eat you up
in one big gulp!

– Please don't eat me!
Wait for my brother:
he is bigger than me... –
cries the little goat.

– All right, you can cross the bridge! – says the giant.

So the second goat arrives.

Clip-clop!
Clip-clop!

– Who's that crossing my bridge? – screams the giant.

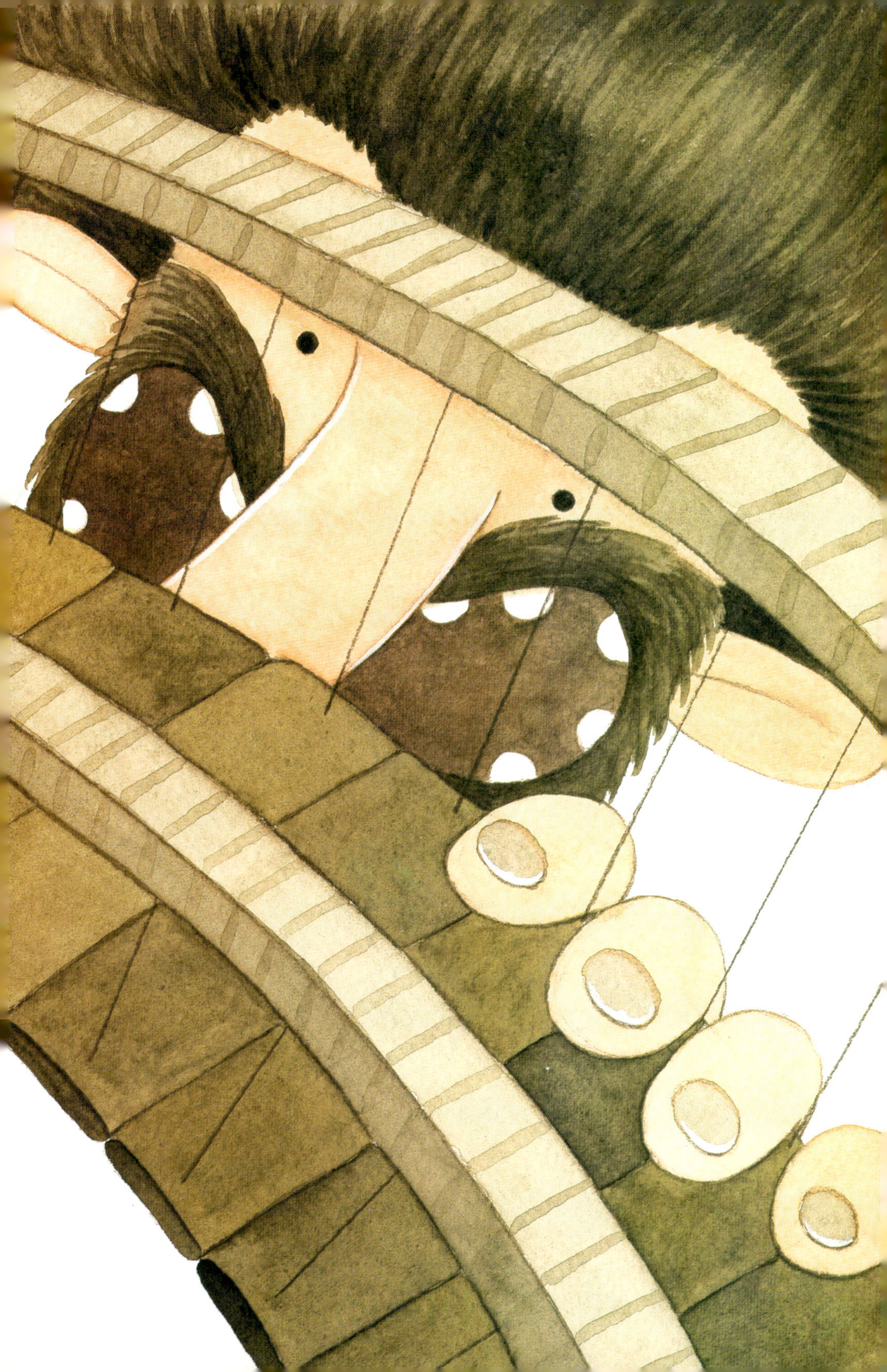

– Billy Goat Gruff – says
the middle-sized goat
in his medium voice.

– I'm going to the field
to eat some grass.

– Oh no, you're not!
I'm going to eat you
up in two big gulps!

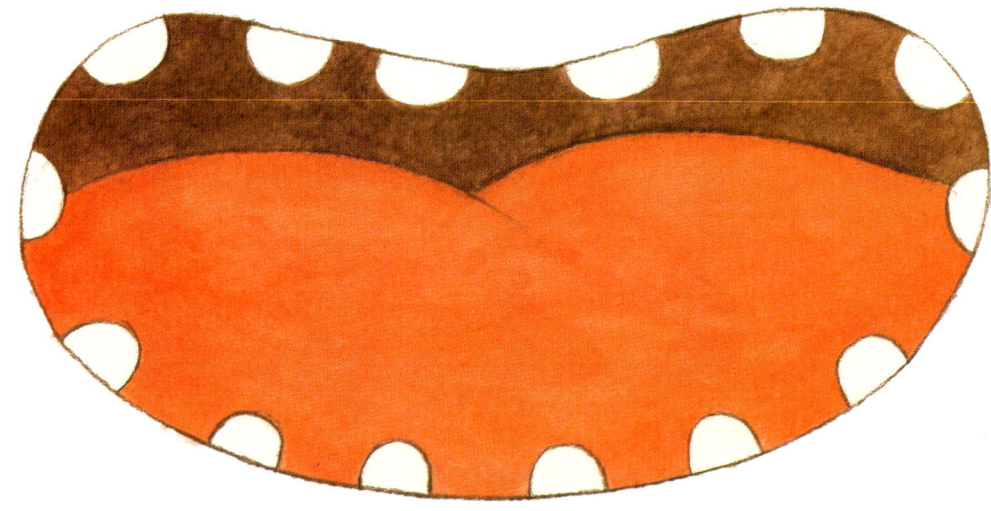

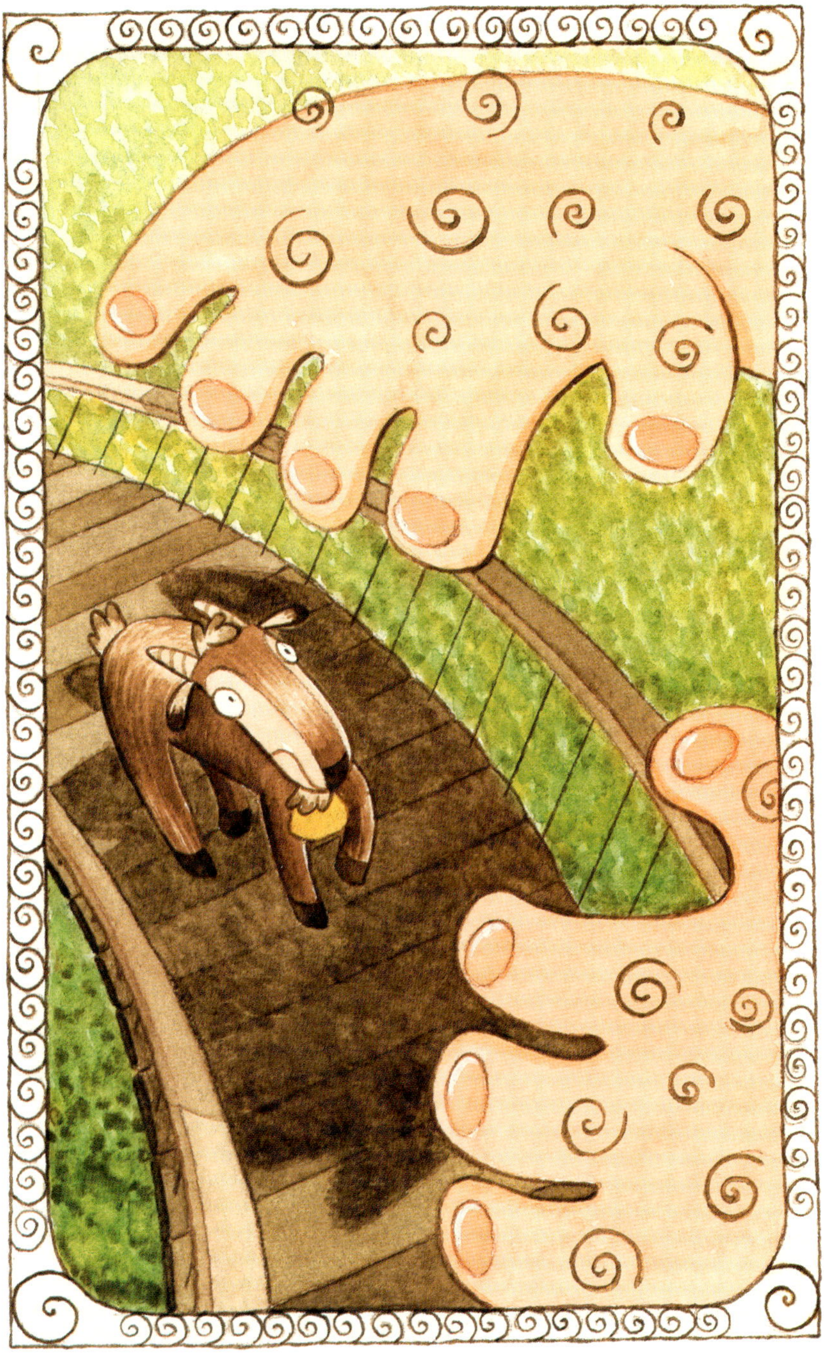

– Please, don't eat me!
Wait for my brother,
who is bigger than me... –
cries the middle-sized goat.

– All right, you can cross the bridge! – says the giant.

The third goat arrives.

Tromp-tramp!
Tromp-tramp!

– Who's that crossing my bridge? – roars the giant.

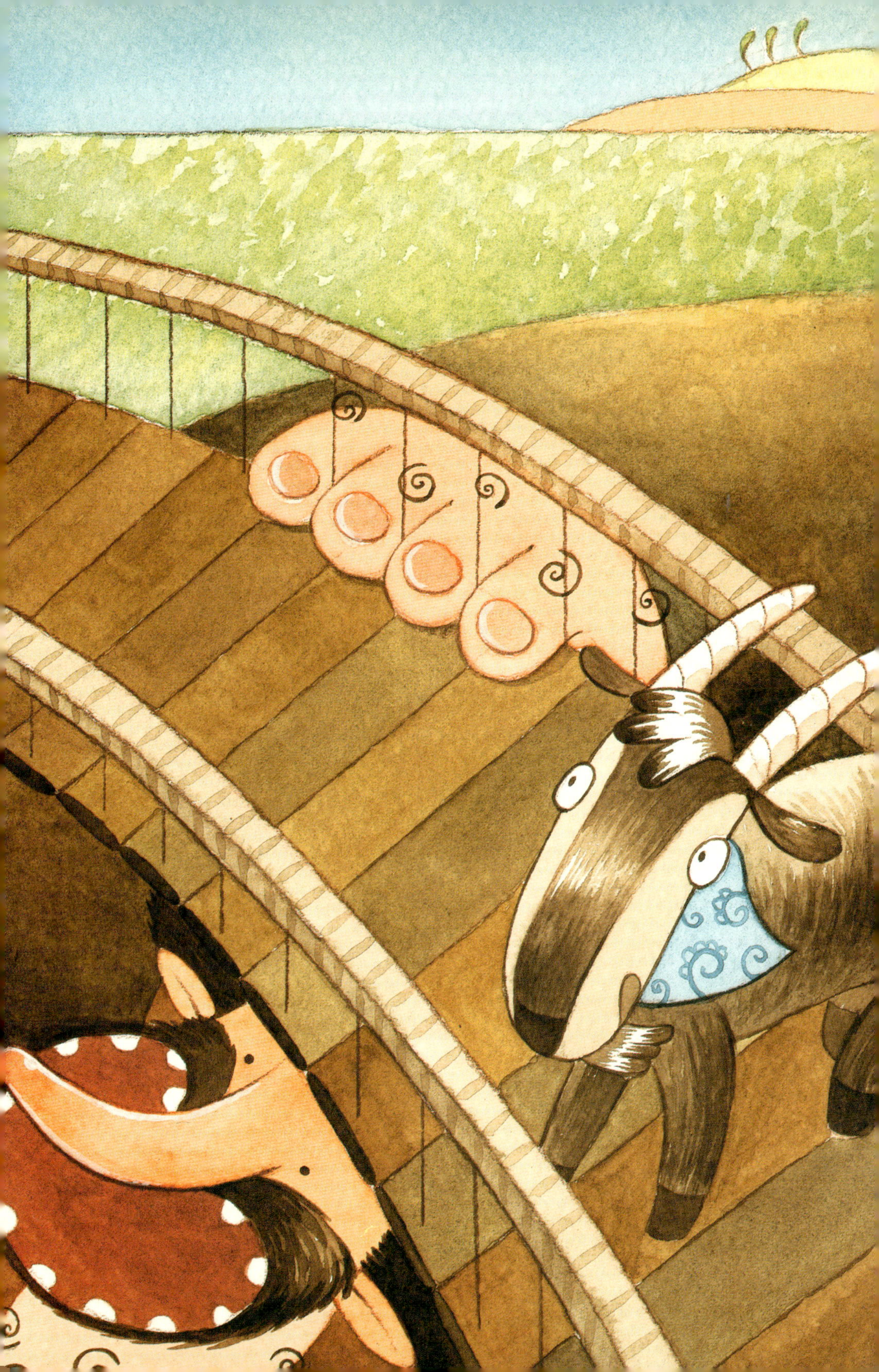

– Billy Goat Gruff – says the big goat in his strong voice.

– I'm going to the field
to eat some grass.

– Oh no, you're not! –
says the giant.
– I'm going to eat you
up in three big gulps!

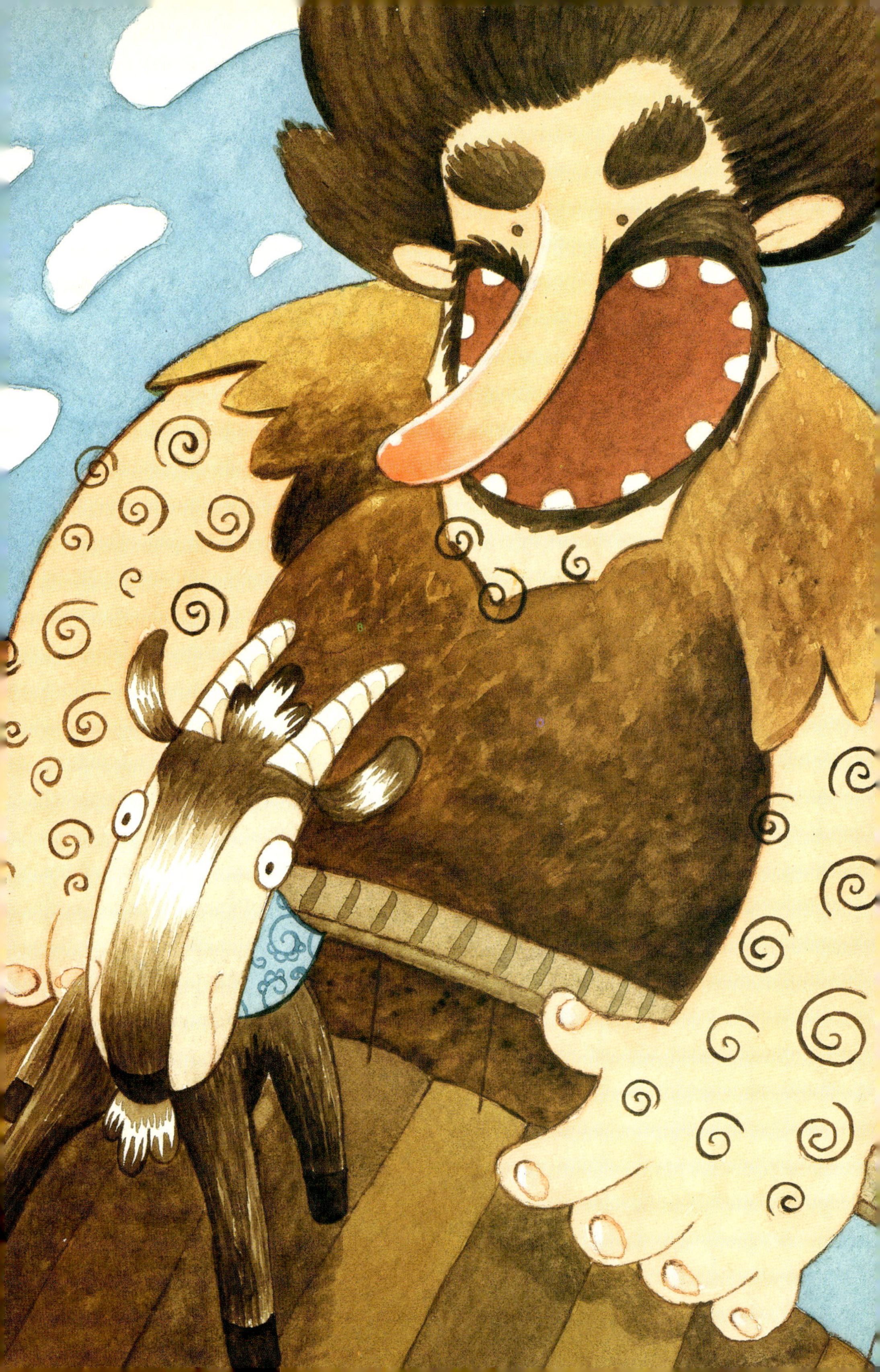

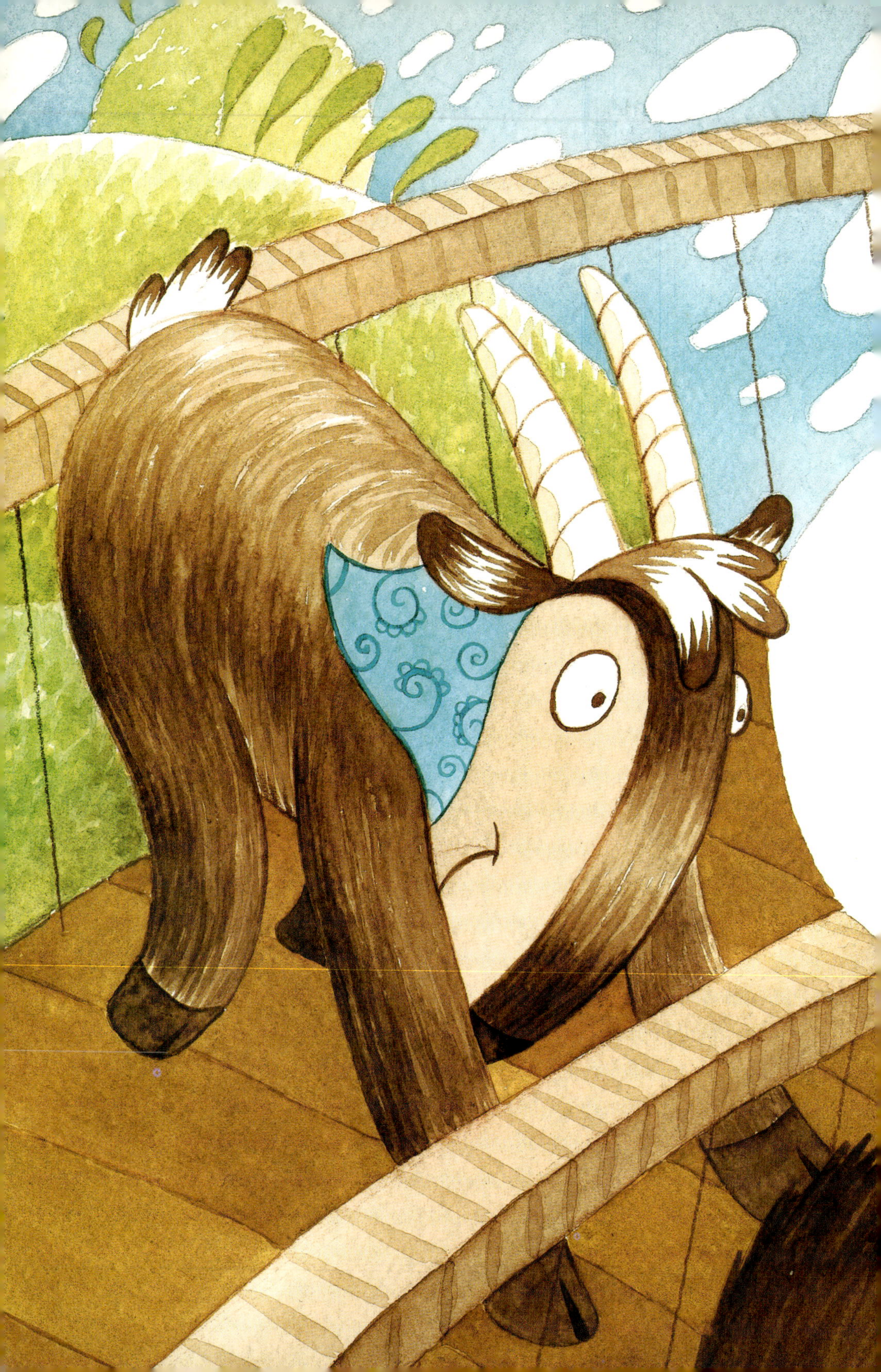

– That's what you think! –
says the big goat.
And…

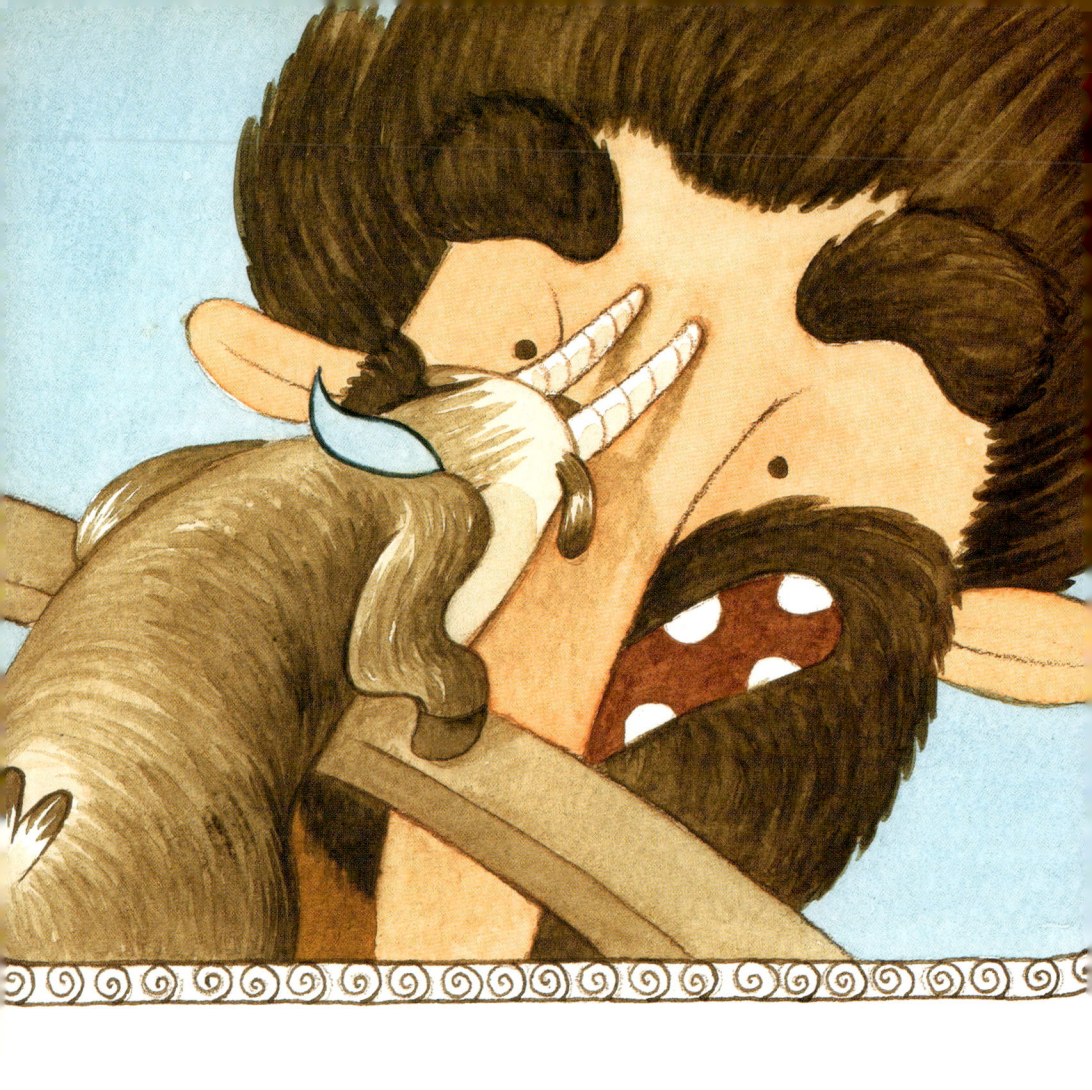

… he lowers his horns
and butts the ugly giant.

Up, up, up flies the giant in the air and…

... down, down, down
goes the giant into
the water below
and disappears.

– Now I'm hungry: I want to eat some grass! – says the big goat.

So, the three
Billy Goats Gruff
eat and eat and eat…

… and they get very, very, very fat!

TRADUZIONE
INGLESE / ITALIANO

I tre capretti furbetti

Pagina 2-3
This is the story of the three Billy Goats Gruff: Big Goat, Middle-sized Goat and Little Goat.

Questa è la storia dei tre Capretti Furbetti: Capretto Grande, Capretto Medio e Capretto Piccolo.

Pagina 4-5
They live in a barn.

Vivono in un fienile.

Pagina 6-7
One day they decide to go and eat some grass in the field.

Un giorno decidono di andare a mangiare un po' d'erba in un prato.

Pagina 8
On the way they have to cross a bridge, but...

Lungo la strada devono attraversare un ponte, ma...

Pagina 9
... under the bridge lives a terrible, ugly giant.

... sotto il ponte vive un brutto e terribile gigante.

Pagina 10
The little Billy Goat Gruff is the first to reach the bridge.

Capretto Piccolo è il primo ad arrivare al ponte.

Pagina 11
Trippity-trop! Trippity-trop!

Trippity-trop! Trippity-trop!

Pagina 12-13
– Who's that crossing my bridge? – growls the giant.

– Chi attraversa il mio ponte? – ringhia il gigante.

Pagina 14
– Billy Goat Gruff – says the little goat in his tiny voice.

– *Un Capretto Furbetto – dice Capretto Piccolo con la sua vocina sottile.*

Pagina 15
– I'm going to the field to eat some grass.

– *Sto andando nel prato a mangiare un po' d'erba.*

Pagina 16-17
– Oh no, you're not! – says the giant.
– I'm going to eat you up in one big gulp!

– *Oh, no che non ci andrai! – dice il gigante.*
– *Ti mangerò in un sol boccone!*

Pagina 18
– Please don't eat me! Wait for my brother: he is bigger than me... – cries the little goat.

– *Ti prego, non mangiarmi! Aspetta mio fratello: lui è più grande di me... – supplica Capretto Piccolo.*

Pagina 19
– All right, you can cross the bridge! – says the giant.

– Va bene, puoi attraversare il ponte! – dice il gigante.

Pagina 20
So the second goat arrives.

Così arriva il secondo capretto.

Pagina 21
Clip-clop! Clip-clop!

Clip-clop! Clip-clop!

Pagina 22-23
– Who's that crossing my bridge? – screams the giant.

– Chi attraversa il mio ponte? – grida il gigante.

Pagina 24
– Billy Goat Gruff – says the middle-sized goat in his medium voice.

– Un Capretto Furbetto – dice Capretto Medio con la sua vocetta un po' più robusta.

Pagina 25
– I'm going to the field to eat some grass.

– *Sto andando nel prato a mangiare un po' d'erba.*

Pagina 26-27
– Oh no, you're not! I'm going to eat you up in two big gulps!

– *Oh, no che non ci andrai! Ti mangerò in due bocconi!*

Pagina 28
– Please, don't eat me! Wait for my brother, who is bigger than me... – cries the middle-sized goat.

– *Ti prego, non mangiarmi! Aspetta mio fratello, che è più grande di me... – supplica Capretto Medio.*

Pagina 29
– All right, you can cross the bridge! – says the giant.

– *Va bene, puoi attraversare il ponte! – dice il gigante.*

Pagina 30
The third goat arrives.

Arriva il terzo capretto.

Pagina 31
Tromp-tramp! Tromp-tramp!

Tromp-tramp! Tromp-tramp!

Pagina 32-33
– Who's that crossing my bridge? – roars the giant.

– Chi attraversa il mio ponte? – ruggisce il gigante.

Pagina 34
– Billy Goat Gruff – says the big goat in his strong voice.

– Un Capretto Furbetto – dice Capretto Grande con la sua voce robusta.

Pagina 35
– I'm going to the field to eat some grass.

– Sto andando nel prato a mangiare un po' d'erba.

Pagina 36-37
– Oh no, you're not! – says the giant.
– I'm going to eat you up in three big gulps!

– Oh, no che non ci andrai! – dice
il gigante.
– Ti mangerò in tre bocconi!

Pagina 38-39
– That's what you think! – says the big goat. And…

– Questo è quello che pensi tu! – dice Capretto Grande. E…

Pagina 40
… he lowers his horns and butts the ugly giant.

… abbassa le corna e colpisce forte il terribile gigante.

Pagina 41
Up, up, up flies the giant in the air and…

Su, su, su vola in aria il gigante e…

Pagina 42
… down, down, down goes the giant into the water below and disappears.

… giù, giù, giù cade il gigante in acqua e scompare.

Pagina 43
– Now I'm hungry: I want to eat some grass! – says the big goat.

– Ora ho fame: voglio mangiare un po' d'erba! – dice Capretto Grande.

Pagina 44
So, the three Billy Goats Gruff eat and eat and eat…

Così i tre Capretti Furbetti mangiano e mangiano e mangiano…

Pagina 45
… and they get very, very, very fat!

… e diventano molto, molto, molto grassi!

Short summary

The three 🐄 live in a 🏠.

They want to eat some 🌿 in the 🌾 but they have to cross a 🌉.

Under the bridge lives an ugly 👹.

The giant wants to eat the 🐐 but decides to wait for his brother

who is bigger then him.
When the 🐐 arrives
the giant decides to wait
for the biggest brother.
The giant wants to eat the
🐐 , but the 🐐
trows the giant up in the air
and down in the 〰️ .
So now the three Billy Goats
Gruff eat so much grass they
get very fat!

Find the Differences

Look carefully at the two pictures
and find out the 5 differences.

*Osserva attentamente le due immagini
e trova le 5 differenze.*

A Wordsearch

Find 4 words of the story!

Trova 4 parole della storia!

GOAT **FIELD**

GRASS **GIANT**

F	I	H	P	S	T
B	F	D	K	N	U
G	I	A	N	T	C
R	E	G	L	Z	O
A	L	T	A	M	E
S	D	V	I	N	P
S	Q	G	O	A	T

What is this?

Join the numbers from one to nine!

Unisci i numeri dall'uno al nove!

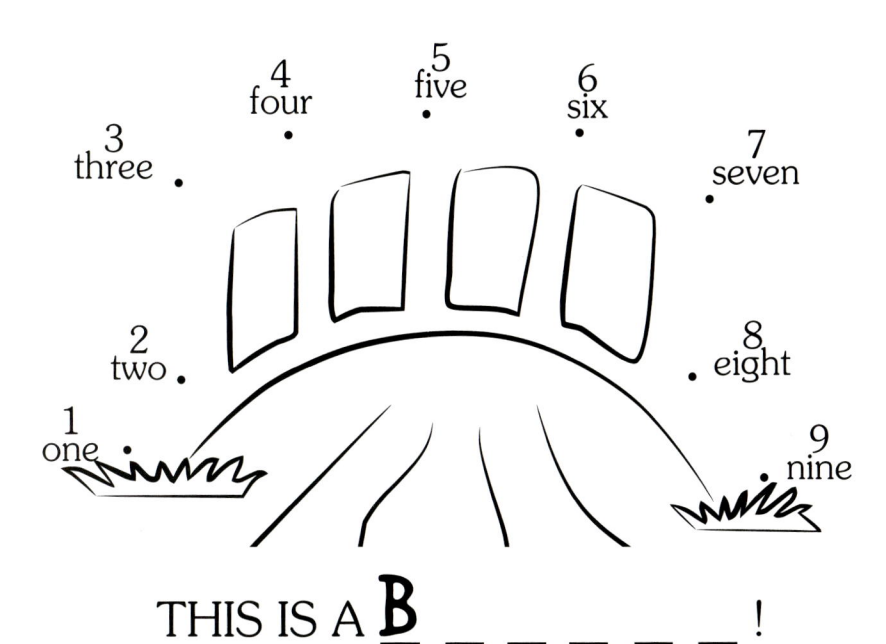

3 three
4 four
5 five
6 six
7 seven
2 two
8 eight
1 one
9 nine

THIS IS A **B** _ _ _ _ _ _ !

Match the Word with the picture!

BIG GOAT

MIDDLE-SIZED GOAT

GIANT

LITTLE GOAT

A Crossword

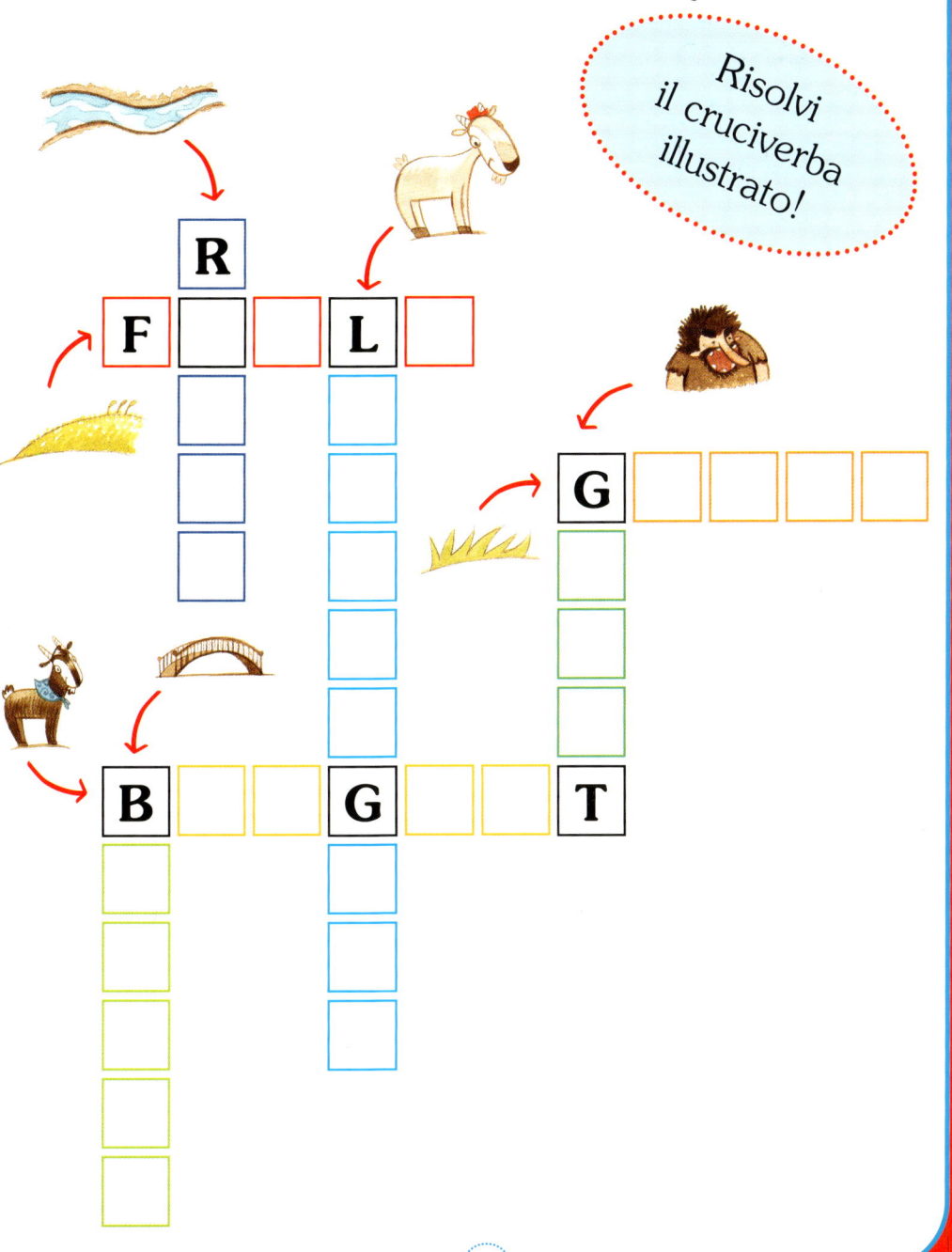

Risolvi il cruciverba illustrato!

A Maze

Help the three Billy Goats Gruff to reach the field!

Aiuta i tre Capretti Furbetti a raggiungere il prato!

A little dictionary

BARN: FIENILE   • • • **sostantivi** • • •
BRIDGE: PONTE
BROTHER: FRATELLO
FIELD: PRATO, PASCOLO
GIANT: GIGANTE
GOAT: CAPRETTO
GRASS: ERBA
GULP: BOCCONE
HORN: CORNO
VOICE: VOCE
WATER: ACQUA
BIG: GRANDE   • • • **aggettivi** • • •
FAT: GRASSO
FIRST: PRIMO
HUNGRY: AFFAMATO
LITTLE: PICCOLO
MIDDLE-SIZED: MEDIO, DI MISURA MEDIA
SECOND: SECONDO
STRONG: FORTE
TERRIBLE: TERRIBILE
THIRD: TERZO

TINY: SOTTILE, PICCINO

UGLY: BRUTTO

••• verbi •••

to **ARRIVE:** ARRIVARE

to **CAN:** POTERE

to **CROSS:** ATTRAVERSARE

to **DISAPPEAR:** SCOMPARIRE

to **EAT:** MANGIARE

to **FLY:** VOLARE

to **GO:** ANDARE

to **GROWL:** BRONTOLARE, RINGHIARE

to **LIVE:** VIVERE

to **REACH:** RAGGIUNGERE

to **ROAR:** RUGGIRE

to **SCREAM:** URLARE

to **THINK:** PENSARE

to **WAIT:** ASPETTARE

A cura di Gabriella Ballarin
Illustrazioni: Maurizia Rubino

www.giunti.it

© 2005 Giunti Editore S.p.A.
Via Bolognese, 165 - 50139 Firenze - Italia
Via Dante, 4 - 20121 Milano - Italia

Ristampa	Anno
6 5 4 3 2 1	2011 2010 2009 2008 2007

Stampato presso Giunti Industrie Grafiche S.p.A. – Stabilimento di Prato